D0646943

KALLA RAE SUSORT

Books by Mary Summer Rain

Nonfiction

Spirit Song
Phoenix Rising
Dreamwalker
Phantoms Afoot
Earthway
Daybreak
Soul Sounds
Whispered Wisdom
Ancient Echoes
Bittersweet
The Visitation
Millennium Memories (Fall '97)

Fiction

The Seventh Mesa

Children's

Mountains, Meadows and Moonbeams
Star Babies (Fall '97)

With Alex Greystone

Mary Summer Rain's Guide to Dream Sumbols

Books on Tape

Spirit Song
Phoenix Rising
Dreamwalker
Phantoms Afoot
The Visitation

STAR BABIES

Mary Summer Rain

For information write:

Hampton Roads Publishing Company, Inc.
134 Burgess Lane
Charlottesville, VA 22902

Or call: (804) 296-2772
FAX: (804) 296-5096
e-mail: hrpc@hrpub.com
Internet: http://www.hrpub.com

If you are unable to order this book from your local
bookseller, you may order directly from the publisher.
Quantity discounts for organizations are available.
Call 1-800-766-8009, toll-free.

Library of Congress Catalog Number: 98-73923

ISBN 1-57174-069-4

10 9 8 7 6 5 4 3 2

Printed on acid-free paper in Canada

Dedicated to the new and enlightened

generation of children who will foster

the understanding that our true reality is

a vast universe peopled with God's children,

that we are all intelligent human beings

sharing one Universe Neighborhood,

and that there is

no such thing as an alien.

STAR BABIES

In the Beginning, when the night sky was first created, God made beautiful galaxies

that circled and spiraled in sparkling ribbons through the heavens.

God made a Blue Star that twinkled like a sapphire gemstone in the sky. This star was mostly all water.

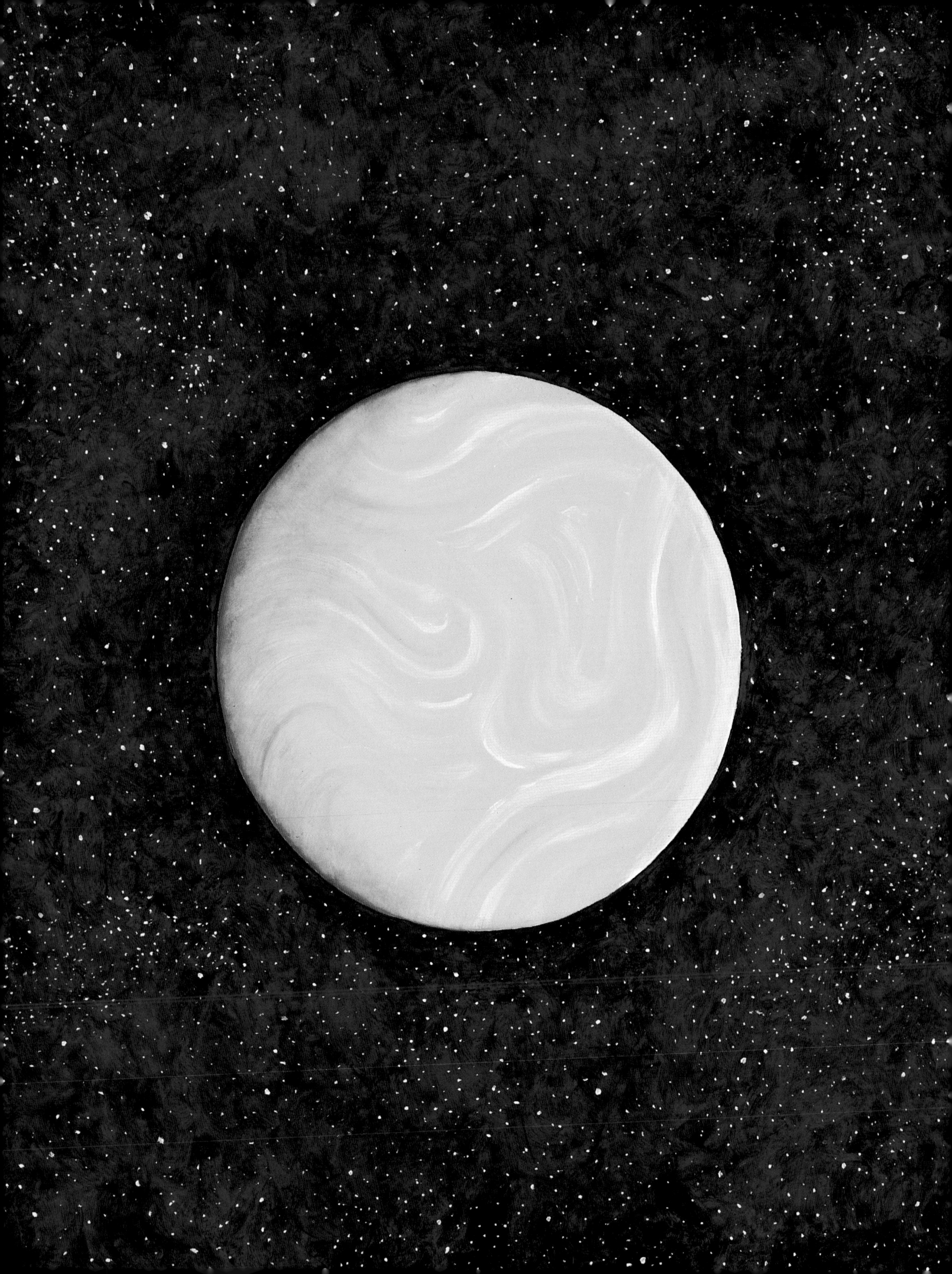

There was a Yellow Star that glistened like shiny gold in the night sky. This star was covered by a vast desert land.

The Purple Star sparkled like an amethyst jewel. It had high misty mountains.

The big Green Star shimmered like a giant emerald set in the sky. This one was covered by lush jungle growth.

Even a Blue and Green Star twinkled as it turned around and around in the heavens.

This Star had deserts, jungles, high mountains, and great oceans of water.

These colored Stars were only a tiny part of the millions and millions of other stars that shimmered as sparkling neighbors to the Milky Way, comets, moons, and suns.

This neighborhood of planets and stars was called Universe. God saw that the Universe Neighborhood was very beautiful. It was good, but it was missing one thing. . .people!

God thought it would be wonderful to have people for some company, so like gently falling rain, millions of living sparkles of God fell like twinkling glitter upon the many stars in the Universe Neighborhood.

And after many, many years went by, each star had people who made their own part of the Universe Neighborhood different in very special ways.

The people on the Blue Star made beautiful underwater crystal cities. They were glad to be a part of God. They loved God very much.

On the Yellow Star, people liked the warmth of the sun. They built high mesa villages. Some were tucked back into the cooling shade of rocks. These people loved God too.

The Purple Star people liked living high up on their mountains because that made them feel closer to God.

In the jungles of the Green Star, great stone pyramids were built. These let the people climb up higher so they could see the other stars in their Universe Neighborhood.

The Blue and Green Star was a little different from the other stars. It was a special blend of all its star neighbors because, a long time ago, people from other planets went there to start their families.

This star had cities and mountain cabins. It had jungle pyramids and desert mesas. But it was the people who made this star extra special. They were different colors and spoke many languages.

God loved the people who lived on all the different stars that made up the Universe Neighborhood.

On the Blue Star the people were very intelligent and gentle. They travelled to neighboring stars and some of their Star Babies had parents from the other stars they frequently visited.

The people on the Yellow Star worked hard to keep their lives simple. This gave them more time to live God's laws and learn from their friends who visited from the Blue Star. Their Star Babies had beautiful golden eyes and were born with many amazing talents.

On the Purple Star, the people worked and played and honored God. They didn't travel to other stars, but when they looked up into the twinkling night sky, they wondered if they had star neighbors they'd someday meet.

These Star Babies had soft lavender eyes and were loved very much.

The Green Star's people worked and played and honored God too. They didn't travel to visit other stars because their star neighbors often came to visit them.

Their Star Babies had sparkling emerald-colored eyes and were sometimes cared for by one of their parents from the Blue Star.

The people on the Blue and Green Star worked, played, and honored God in many, many different ways. They traveled as far as their moon.

Some of these people believed that they had star neighbors. Some didn't believe. They called their star Earth and their Star Babies looked just like. . .

. . .YOU!

***You* are a Star Child too!**

Hampton Roads Publishing Company

. . .for the evolving human spirit

Hampton Roads Publishing Company
publishes and distributes books on a variety of subjects,
including metaphysics, health, complementary medicine,
visionary fiction and other related topics.

To order or receive a copy of our latest catalog, call toll-free,
(800) 766-8009, or send your name and address to:

Hampton Roads Publishing Company, Inc.
134 Burgess Lane
Charlottesville, VA 22902

This edition published by Parragon Books Ltd in 2013
and distributed by

Parragon Inc.
440 Park Avenue South, 13th Floor
New York, NY 10016
www.parragon.com

Written by Peter Bently
Illustrated by Deborah Melmon

ISBN 978-1-4723-3609-5

Printed In China

UNDERPANTS
WONDERPANTS
Parragon
Bath • New York • Singapore • Hong Kong • Cologne • Delhi
Melbourne • Amsterdam • Johannesburg • Shenzhen

Is it an eagle?

Is it a plane?

NO—it's Underpants Wonderpants
to the **rescue** again!

Whenever you
need him,
in sun,
snow,
or shower,

he'll **fix** all your

problems with

UNDERPANTS POWER!

"Elephant **sat** on our nest!"

grumbles Mouse.

"No problem!" says **WONDERPANTS.**

ZAP!

An **underpants** house!

Polar Bear Cub
can't keep up in the **storm.**

ZAP!
Thanks to **Wonderpants** she's **cozy**
and **warm!**

Kangaroo cries,

"I've been **itching** all night!"

ZAP!

In this hammock, the insects can't **bite**!

The fisherman's
ripped a **big** hole
in his net. **ZAP!**

“Thank you, **WONDERPANTS!**
It’s my **biggest** catch yet!”

"Help!" cries the Queen.
It's so far to the ground–

Wonderpants' Pantachute helps her land **safe** and **sound!**

Wonderpants **zooms** to the river,
and in a **great swoop**–

he puts out the **fire** with his

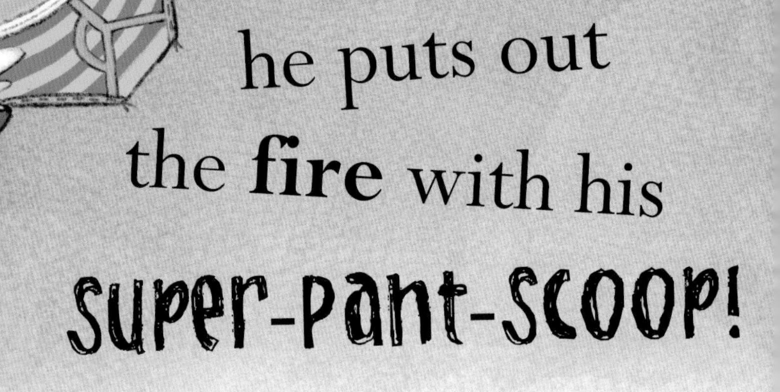

SUPER-PANT-SCOOP!

But that's not the **end** of his super-pants day ...

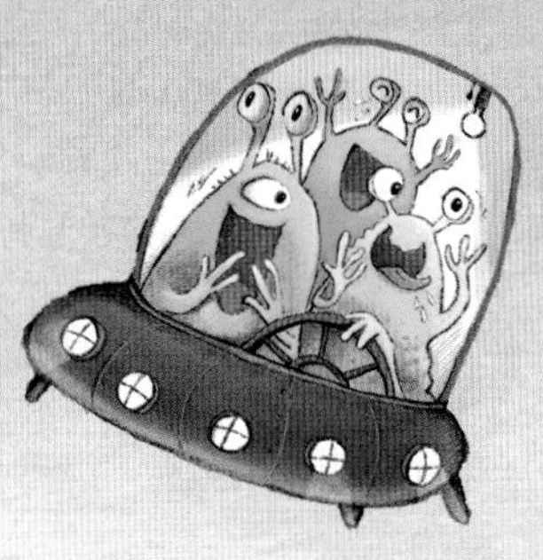

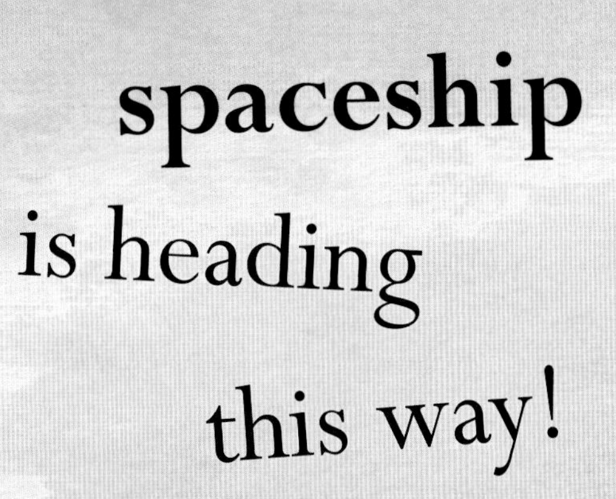

An **alien**

spaceship

is heading

this way!

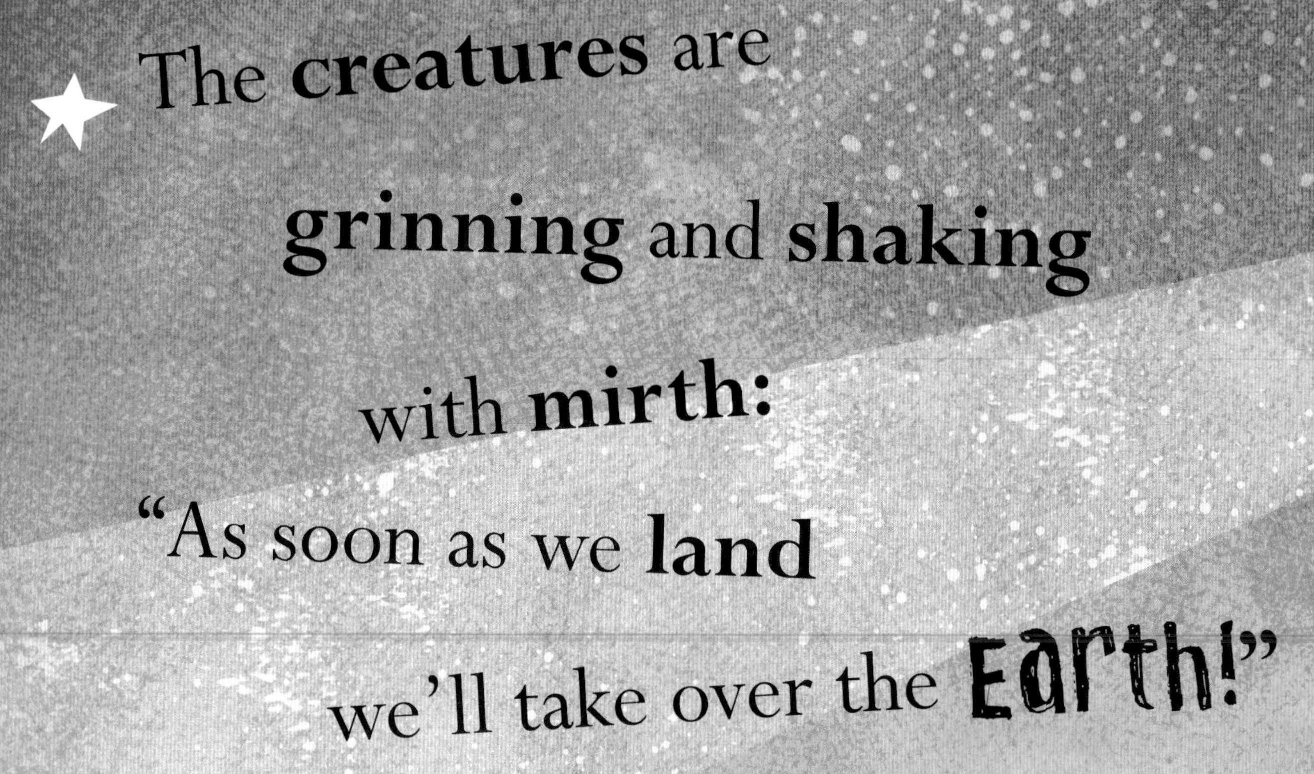

The **creatures** are
grinning and **shaking**
with **mirth:**
"As soon as we **land**
we'll take over the **Earth!**"

But **imagine** the look on
each **alien's** face

when a **WONDERPANTS**

sling sends them—**ZAP!**—back to **space!**

The people all **cheer**

as they **watch** from afar:

"**WONDERPANTS**

saved us all—

"He's our

SUPER-PANTS STAR!"